VICENZA TRAVEL GUIDE

2024

Your Essential Travel Companion - From Planning to Exploring.

GARFIELD JAMES

TABLE OF CONTENTS

INTRODUCTIONS

Vicenza, a city nestled in the foothills of northern Italy's Veneto region, is more than just a charming Italian town. It's an open-air museum, a testament to artistic genius, and a vibrant hub where history whispers from every corner.

A City Steeped in History

Vicenza's story stretches back centuries, with Roman roots evident in its urban layout. Conquered by various empires, the city absorbed influences from each era, leaving behind a rich tapestry woven with elements of Romanesque, Gothic, and Renaissance styles. However, it was the arrival of a young stonemason named Andrea Palladio in the 16th century that truly transformed Vicenza.

Palladio's Playground: A Renaissance Masterpiece

Palladio, with his revolutionary approach to classical architecture, found his artistic haven in Vicenza. Inspired by the ancient world, he designed buildings that embodied elegance, proportion, and harmony. From the iconic Basilica Palladiana with its grand loggias to the intimate Teatro Olimpico, the city became a living showcase of Palladian genius.

Beyond Palladio: A City Alive

While Palladio's legacy remains the cornerstone of Vicenza's charm, the city offers much more to the discerning traveler.Piazza dei Signori, the beating heart of Vicenza, pulsates with life. Here, you can admire the elegant Palazzo del Capitano or simply relax under the shade of arcades, sipping a cup of espresso and soaking in the atmosphere. The majestic Cathedral (Duomo) and the captivating Teatro Rossi, a haven for opera lovers, stand as testaments to Vicenza's rich artistic heritage.

A Culinary Adventure Awaits

Vicenza's culinary scene is a delightful surprise. Fresh, seasonal ingredients take center stage, with dishes reflecting the region's agricultural bounty. Sample mouthwatering risottos, savor the delicate flavors of "Bigoli" (thick spaghetti) with ragù, or indulge in the local specialty, "Baccalà alla Vicentina" (salted codfish). From cozy osterias to Michelin-starred restaurants, Vicenza caters to every taste and budget.

A Gateway to Exploration

Vicenza's strategic location makes it an ideal base for exploring the Veneto region. Take a day trip to the romantic city of Verona, the setting for Shakespeare's Romeo and Juliet. Immerse yourself in the historical and artistic treasures of Padua,home to Saint Anthony's Basilica and a vibrant university town. Explore the rolling hills of the region's wine country,dotted with charming vineyards and offering delectable local wines.

Or venture beyond the city walls to discover the Palladian villas scattered across the countryside, each a masterpiece in its own right.

A City for All Seasons

Whether you seek the cultural richness of spring and summer, the vibrant colors of autumn, or the festive charm of winter,Vicenza offers a unique experience. From the joyous celebration of Carnival to the prestigious Vicenza Gold Fair showcasing Italian jewelry craftsmanship, the city's calendar is dotted with events that cater to diverse interests.

Unforgettable Experiences Await

Vicenza is a city that lingers in your memory long after you leave. It's a place where history whispers through ancient walls, where artistic masterpieces grace every corner, and where the warmth of Italian hospitality makes you feel right at home. So pack your bags, embrace the spirit of discovery, and embark on an unforgettable journey to Vicenza – a city where beauty and history collide in a truly captivating way.

Chapter one

Welcome to Vicenza - A Brief History and Overview

Vicenza, a jewel nestled in the Veneto region of northern Italy, beckons travelers with its rich history, architectural wonders, and captivating charm. This city, embraced by the foothills of the Lessini Mountains, offers a unique blend of cultural experiences, from exploring the masterpieces of Renaissance architect Andrea Palladio to indulging in the region's delectable cuisine.

A Journey Through Time: Vicenza's Historical Tapestry

Vicenza's story begins over two millennia ago. Founded by the Romans in 148 BC as Vicetia, the city served as a strategic military outpost. Evidence of this Roman past can still be seen in the city's orthogonal layout, a testament to Roman engineering. After the fall of the Roman Empire, Vicenza witnessed a period of turmoil, changing hands between various powers, including the Lombards and the Franks.

The arrival of the Scaligeri family in the 13th century marked a period of relative stability and prosperity. The Scaligeri,known for their patronage of the arts, left their mark on the city's architecture, most notably with the construction of the Castelvecchio, a powerful castle that still stands today.

However, it was the 15th century that ushered in a golden age for Vicenza. The city fell under the rule of the Republic of Venice, a period marked by economic growth and artistic flourishing. Venetian influence is evident in the elegant architecture of Piazza dei Signori, the heart of the city, and the construction of the imposing Basilica Palladiana.

Palladio's Legacy: A City Transformed

But the true architect of Vicenza's modern identity is Andrea Palladio. This young stonemason, born in Padua in 1508,arrived in Vicenza in the mid-16th century. Inspired by the classical world, Palladio developed a revolutionary approach to architecture, emphasizing symmetry, proportion, and the integration of classical elements. Vicenza became his canvas,a stage upon which he showcased his genius.

From the iconic Basilica Palladiana, a masterpiece of public architecture, to the intimate Teatro Olimpico, the world's oldest indoor theater, Palladian buildings graced the city. Private mansions, known as palazzos, commissioned by wealthy Vicentine families like the Chiericati and the Valmarana, further solidified Palladio's influence. His work not only transformed the city's skyline but also established Vicenza as a center of Renaissance architectural innovation.

Beyond Palladio: A City Vibrant and Diverse

While Palladio's legacy remains the cornerstone of Vicenza's artistic identity, the city offers a wealth of experiences beyond his architectural masterpieces. Stepping into Piazza dei Signori is like stepping back in time. Here, the imposing Palazzo del Capitano, once the seat of Venetian power, stands opposite the Basilica Palladiana. Arcades lined with shops and cafes provide a shady haven to relax and soak in the atmosphere.

The majestic Cathedral (Duomo), a stunning example of Gothic architecture, stands as a testament to Vicenza's rich religious heritage. Music lovers can pay homage to the art of opera at the Teatro Rossi, a 18th-century theater renowned for its acoustics and elegant interiors.

A Culinary Paradise Awaits

Vicenza's culinary scene is a delightful surprise, offering a delicious exploration of the region's agricultural bounty. Fresh,seasonal ingredients take center stage in local dishes, with a focus on simplicity and flavor. Sample mouthwatering risottos prepared with local cheeses and vegetables, savor the delicate flavors of "Bigoli" (thick spaghetti) with ragù, or indulge in the local specialty, "Baccalà alla Vicentina" (salted codfish) – a dish steeped in tradition.

From cozy osterias tucked away in narrow streets to Michelin-starred restaurants serving innovative takes on regional cuisine, Vicenza caters to every taste and budget. Don't miss the chance to explore the city's vibrant food markets, where you can find everything from fresh produce and local cheeses to cured meats and artisanal breads.

A Gateway to Exploration

Vicenza's strategic location makes it an ideal base for exploring the Veneto region. Take a day trip to the romantic city of Verona, where Shakespeare's Romeo and Juliet set the stage for their tragic love story. Immerse yourself in the historical and artistic treasures of Padua, a vibrant university town known for Saint Anthony's Basilica and its Giotto frescoes.

Venture beyond the city walls and explore the rolling hills of the region's wine country, dotted with charming vineyards offering delectable local wines like Valpolicella and Soave. Discover the Palladian villas scattered across the countryside,each a masterpiece of Renaissance architecture designed by Palladio himself. These villas, like the Villa Rotonda or the Villa Valmarana ai Nani, offer a glimpse into the lives of the Venetian aristocracy and a chance to experience Palladio's genius in a more intimate setting.

A City for All Seasons

Vicenza offers a unique experience throughout the year. Spring brings a vibrant energy to the city as the weather warms and outdoor cafes come alive. Explore the city on foot or rent a bike to meander through charming streets adorned with blooming flowers.

Summer transforms Vicenza into a bustling hub of activity. Piazza dei Signori becomes a stage for open-air concerts and cultural events. Escape the midday heat by exploring the cool interiors of the Civic Museums or the Palazzo Chiericati,which houses a renowned collection of Venetian paintings.

Autumn paints the city in warm hues of orange, red, and yellow. Take a stroll through the Giardini Salvi, a beautiful public garden offering a peaceful escape from the city center. Food lovers can rejoice during the autumn harvest festivals,where local producers showcase their seasonal bounty.

Winter brings a festive charm to Vicenza. The city transforms into a wonderland of twinkling lights and Christmas markets offering traditional crafts and delicious treats. Immerse yourself in the joyous atmosphere of Carnival, a celebration filled with colorful costumes, parades, and masked balls.

A City of Events and Celebrations

Vicenza's calendar is dotted with events that cater to diverse interests. History buffs can't miss the Palladio Festival, a celebration of the life and work of the city's most famous architect. Held annually, the festival offers lectures, exhibitions,and performances that delve into Palladio's legacy.

Jewelry enthusiasts flock to the Vicenza Gold Fair, a prestigious international event showcasing the finest Italian jewelry craftsmanship. Music lovers can indulge in a variety of concerts and operas throughout the year, from classical performances at the Teatro Olimpico to contemporary music festivals held in various venues across the city.

Planning Your Vicenza Adventure

Whether you're a history buff, an architecture enthusiast, or simply a curious traveler seeking a charming Italian getaway,Vicenza has something to offer everyone. With its rich heritage, captivating sights, and delectable cuisine, Vicenza promises an unforgettable journey. This chapter has provided a brief overview of the city's history and what awaits you. In the following chapters, we'll delve deeper into specific aspects of Vicenza, helping you plan your perfect trip.

Unveiling Vicenza's charm - From Roman roots to Palladian masterpiece

Vicenza, a captivating city nestled in the foothills of northern Italy's Veneto region, boasts a charm that transcends time.its story, woven with threads of Roman engineering, medieval grandeur, and Renaissance artistry, unfolds on every corner you turn. This chapter delves into the captivating history that shaped Vicenza, transforming it from a Roman outpost to a city adorned with Palladian masterpieces.
A Walk Through Time: Unveiling Vicenza's Roman Legacy

The story of Vicenza begins over two millennia ago, around 148 BC. The Romans, renowned for their strategic prowess,established a military outpost called Vicetia. This early settlement laid the foundation for the city's urban layout,characterized by a grid of intersecting streets – a testament to Roman planning and engineering expertise. Even today,remnants of the Roman era can be found scattered throughout the city.

Venture underground to explore the fascinating ruins of the Cryptoporticus, an underground passageway used for storage and transportation during Roman times. Step into the Museo Civico Archeologico, where artifacts whisper tales of Vicenza's Roman past. Admire the imposing Berga Tower (Torre Bissara), a remnant of the city's Roman walls, offering a panoramic view of the city below.

From Medieval Majesty to Venetian Grandeur
Following the fall of the Roman Empire, Vicenza entered a period of uncertainty. The city changed hands numerous times, witnessing the rule of Lombards, Franks, and ultimately, the Scaligeri family in the 13th century. The Scaligeri,known for their patronage of the arts, left their mark on Vicenza's architecture. The imposing Castelvecchio, a powerful castle with its distinctive swallow-tailed merlons, stands as a symbol of their rule.

The 15th century marked a turning point in Vicenza's history. The city fell under the dominion of the powerful Republic of Venice, ushering in an era of economic prosperity and artistic flourishing. Venetian influence is evident in the elegant architecture of Piazza dei Signori, the heart of the city. Here, the imposing Basilica Palladiana, originally designed as a marketplace but never completed, reflects the Venetian Gothic style with its pointed arches and decorative details. The Venetian Loggia, a refined structure adorned with marble columns and sculptures, embodies the grandeur and artistic sensibilities of the Venetian Republic.
The Arrival of Palladio: A Renaissance Masterpiece Emerges

However, the true architect of Vicenza's modern identity arrived in the mid-16th century. Andrea Palladio, a young stonemason with a passion for classical architecture, arrived in Vicenza in 1546. Inspired by the ideals of ancient Greece and Rome, Palladio developed a revolutionary approach to architecture. He emphasized symmetry, proportion, and the integration of classical elements like columns, pediments, and arches into his designs.

Vicenza became Palladio's canvas, a stage upon which he showcased his genius. The city council, recognizing Palladio's talent, entrusted him with the task of renovating the Basilica Palladiana. Palladio transformed the unfinished structure,adding the iconic loggias (arcades) that define its facade today. This project marked the beginning of a fruitful collaboration that would forever alter Vicenza's skyline.

A City Transformed: A Legacy in Stone
Palladio's influence extended far beyond the Basilica Palladiana. He designed numerous private mansions, known as palazzos, for wealthy Vicentine families. These palazzos, like the Palazzo Chiericati and the Palazzo Valmarana,embodied Palladio's architectural principles. Their elegant facades, featuring symmetrical layouts, rhythmic columns, and grand staircases, became testaments to Palladian mastery.

Palladio's impact wasn't limited to just the city center. He ventured beyond the city walls, designing villas for the Venetian aristocracy scattered across the surrounding

16

countryside. These villas, like the Villa Rotonda (La Rotonda) and the Villa Valmarana ai Nani (Villa with Dwarfs), showcased Palladio's versatility and ability to adapt his style to different settings.These structures, with their perfect proportions and harmonious integration into the landscape, became iconic examples of Palladian architecture.

Beyond Palladio: A Tapestry of Architectural Delights

While Palladio's legacy remains the cornerstone of Vicenza's artistic identity, the city boasts a wealth of architectural delights beyond his masterpieces. Stepping into Piazza dei Signori is like stepping back in time. The Palazzo del Capitano, once the seat of Venetian power, stands opposite the Basilica Palladiana. The Gothic-style Cathedral (Duomo) with its soaring bell tower offers a counterpoint to the Palladian structures. The Teatro Olimpico, the world's oldest indoor theater, designed by Palladio himself, stands as a testament to the city's rich theatrical heritage.Exploring these diverse architectural styles reveals the multifaceted history of Vicenza, where each era has left its mark on the city's fabric.

A Legacy that Endures: Vicenza Today

Vicenza's architectural heritage continues to shape its present. The city's historic center, a UNESCO World Heritage Site,is a living museum, where ancient streets wind past Renaissance palaces and Gothic churches. These structures,meticulously restored, house museums, art galleries, and shops, breathing new life into the city's past.

17

The influence of Palladio extends beyond the physical structures. His architectural principles continue to inspire contemporary architects and urban planners worldwide. The Vicenza Institute, a prestigious architectural school, carries the torch of Palladianism, promoting the study and application of his ideas in the modern world.

Experiencing Palladio's Masterpieces

No visit to Vicenza is complete without immersing yourself in the world of Palladio. Start your exploration at the Palladio Museum, housed in the Palazzo Barbarano. Here, interactive exhibits and detailed models bring Palladio's life and work to life. Step into the Basilica Palladiana and wander through the elegant loggias, each offering a unique perspective of the city below.

Next, head to the Teatro Olimpico, a marvel of Renaissance stage design. This permanent, indoor theater, designed by Palladio and completed by his son Scamozzi, is the oldest surviving theater in the world. Take a guided tour to marvel at the trompe-l'œil scenery that creates the illusion of a seemingly endless street stretching into the distance.

Venture beyond the city center and explore the Palladian villas scattered across the countryside. The Villa Rotonda, with its symmetrical design and dome perched atop a cylindrical core, embodies Palladio's fascination with classical forms.The Villa Valmarana ai Nani, adorned with whimsical dwarf statues, offers a more playful side of Palladian architecture.

A City Beyond Architecture

While architecture is undeniably Vicenza's crown jewel, the city offers much more. Explore the bustling food markets,overflowing with fresh produce and local delicacies. Immerse yourself in the city's vibrant cultural scene, with museums showcasing everything from ancient Roman artifacts to contemporary art. Relax in charming cafes and sip on a cup of espresso as you soak in the atmosphere.

Vicenza's charm lies in the harmonious blend of its rich history, architectural wonders, and vibrant present. From the Roman foundations to the Palladian masterpieces, the city tells a captivating story waiting to be discovered. So, pack your bags and embark on a journey to Vicenza, a place where history whispers from every corner, and Palladio's legacy continues to inspire.

A city for all seasons - When to visit Vicenza

Vicenza, a captivating city nestled amidst the rolling hills of northern Italy's Veneto region, welcomes visitors with open arms throughout the year. Each season offers a unique experience, catering to diverse preferences. Whether you crave the vibrancy of summer festivals or the tranquility of a winter wonderland, Vicenza has something special in store for you.

Spring (March to May): A City Awakens

Spring paints Vicenza in a palette of vibrant colors. As the days lengthen and temperatures rise, the city awakens from its winter slumber. Lush greenery replaces the bare winter branches, and colorful blooms adorn balconies and courtyards.

Ideal for: Outdoor enthusiasts, art lovers, budget travelers

Why Spring is Special:

Pleasant weather: Spring offers a delightful escape from the summer heat and the winter chill. Temperatures are comfortable for exploring the city on foot or by bike.

Blooming landscapes: Witness the city adorned with vibrant flowers, adding a touch of magic to every corner.

Fewer crowds: Spring offers a more relaxed atmosphere compared to the peak summer season. Enjoy shorter lines at museums and attractions.

Travel to Vicenza 2024

Lower accommodation rates: Hotel rates tend to be lower compared to the peak season, making spring an attractive option for budget travelers.

Things to Do in Spring:

Explore the city: Stroll through the charming streets of the historic center, admiring the architectural gems like the Basilica Palladiana and the Piazza dei Signori.

Visit the Giardini Salvi: Escape the hustle and bustle of the city center and relax in the peaceful Giardini Salvi, a delightful public garden.

Catch an outdoor concert: Spring brings numerous outdoor events to life, from classical music concerts in the piazzas to traditional folk festivals.

Explore the Palladian Villas: With the pleasant weather, spring is an ideal time to venture beyond the city walls and explore the captivating Palladian villas scattered across the surrounding countryside.

Art Exhibitions: Spring often sees the opening of new exhibitions at the city's museums, offering a chance to delve deeper into Vicenza's rich artistic heritage.

Summer (June to August): A Buzzing Hub of Activity

Summer transforms Vicenza into a vibrant hub of activity. The city pulsates with energy as locals and tourists alike bask in the warm sunshine. Piazza dei

Signori becomes a stage for open-air concerts, street performers, and lively outdoor cafes.

Ideal for: Festival enthusiasts, history buffs, foodies

Why Summer is Special:

Long sunny days: Make the most of the extended daylight hours to explore the city's attractions and soak up the Italian sunshine.

Outdoor festivals: Summer is jam-packed with exciting festivals, including the Vicenza Gold Fair, showcasing the finest Italian jewelry craftsmanship, and the Palladio Festival, a celebration of the life and work of the city's most famous architect.

Evening strolls: As the sun sets, the city transforms into a magical landscape, with buildings bathed in warm light.Enjoy a leisurely evening stroll through the charming streets.

Culinary Delights: Summer offers the perfect opportunity to explore Vicenza's vibrant outdoor food markets,overflowing with fresh seasonal produce, and indulge in delectable al fresco dining experiences.

Things to Do in Summer:

Visit the Teatro Olimpico: Witness a performance at the world's oldest indoor theater, a marvel of Renaissance stage design.

Explore the museums: Escape the midday heat by delving into Vicenza's rich history and artistic heritage at the Civic Museums or the Palazzo Chiericati.

Take a day trip: With its strategic location, Vicenza makes a perfect base for exploring the surrounding region.Visit the romantic city of Verona or immerse yourself in the historical treasures of Padua.

Wine tasting tours: Embark on a journey through the rolling hills of the Veneto wine region, sampling delectable local wines like Valpolicella and Soave.

Enjoy an opera under the stars: Immerse yourself in the magic of opera during a performance held in an open-air venue under the starlit sky.

Fall (September to November): A Season of Tranquility

As summer fades, Vicenza embraces a season of tranquility. The scorching heat gives way to comfortable temperatures,ideal for outdoor exploration. Fall paints the city in a palette of warm hues, with leaves turning golden and red, adding a touch of romance to the atmosphere.

Ideal for: Nature lovers, budget travelers, photography enthusiasts

Why Fall is Special:

Pleasant weather: Fall offers a comfortable escape from the summer heat, perfect for exploring the city on foot or by bike.

Reduced crowds: Enjoy the city's attractions without the summer bustle.

Lower accommodation rates: Hotel rates typically decrease after the peak summer season, making fall a budget-friendly time to visit.

Things to Do in Fall:

Explore the Giardini Salvi: Witness the transformation of the Giardini Salvi as the leaves change color, creating a breathtaking autumnal spectacle.

Food and Wine Festivals: Fall brings a celebration of the seasonal harvest. Immerse yourself in the vibrant local food and wine festivals, savoring traditional dishes and sampling the latest vintages from the region.

Bike tours: With the comfortable temperatures, fall offers a perfect opportunity to explore Vicenza and its surrounding countryside on a leisurely bike tour.

Learn about Palladio: Participate in workshops or lectures offered by the Palladio Institute, delving deeper into the life and work of the city's most famous architect.

Capture the autumn colors: Fall offers a photographer's paradise. Capture the city's architectural wonders bathed in the warm hues of the season.

Winter (December to February): A Festive Charm

Winter transforms Vicenza into a magical wonderland. The city embraces a festive atmosphere with twinkling lights adorning streets and squares. Christmas markets brim with traditional crafts and delicious treats, offering a warm and inviting atmosphere.

Ideal for: Budget travelers, Christmas enthusiasts, romantic getaways

Why Winter is Special:

Reduced crowds: Enjoy the city's charm without the summer crowds, allowing you to explore at your own pace.

Lower accommodation rates: Hotel rates are typically at their lowest during the winter season, making Vicenza an attractive option for budget travelers.

Festive charm: Immerse yourself in the magic of Christmas, with carols filling the air and Christmas markets offering unique gifts and delectable treats.

Romantic atmosphere: The quiet city streets and cozy cafes create a perfect setting for a romantic getaway.

Things to Do in Winter:

Christmas markets: Explore the enchanting Christmas markets, browsing through artisan crafts, festive decorations, and indulging in traditional local treats like Panettone (sweet bread) and Vin Brulè (mulled wine).

Carnival: Witness the vibrant celebration of Carnival, filled with colorful costumes, parades, and masked balls.

Museums and art galleries: Escape the winter chill by exploring the city's rich cultural offerings at the Civic Museums, the Palazzo Chiericati, or the Palladio Museum.

Opera performances: Winter offers numerous opera performances held at the Teatro Olimpico or other venues,providing a unique cultural experience.

Warm Vicentine hospitality: Seek refuge from the cold in cozy osterias and restaurants, experiencing the warmth of Vicentine hospitality and indulging in hearty winter dishes.

Choosing the Perfect Time to Visit Vicenza

No matter the season, Vicenza offers a unique and unforgettable experience. Spring beckons with its blooming landscapes and relaxed atmosphere. Summer brings vibrant festivals and ideal weather for exploring the city's treasures. Fall enchants with its warm colors and harvest celebrations. Winter transforms Vicenza into a magical wonderland, perfect for a romantic getaway or a festive escape. Ultimately, the best time to visit Vicenza depends on your individual preferences and interests. So, pack your bags, consider the experiences you seek, and set out to discover the captivating charm of Vicenza, a city that welcomes visitors with open arms throughout the year.

Getting to Vicenza - Transportation options by air, train, and car

Vicenza, a treasure trove of history, architecture, and culture, beckons travelers from around the world. But before you embark on your Italian adventure, navigating the transportation options is crucial. This chapter delves into the various ways to reach Vicenza, ensuring a smooth and stress-free journey.

Flying High: Arriving by Air

While Vicenza doesn't have its own airport, several nearby airports offer convenient connections to the city.

Verona Airport (VRN): Located approximately 60 kilometers from Vicenza, Verona Airport is the closest major airport. Several airlines operate flights here, particularly from European destinations. Upon arrival in Verona, you can easily reach Vicenza by train or bus. The train journey takes around 25-40 minutes, while the bus ride is slightly longer, at about an hour.

Venice Marco Polo Airport (VCE): Venice Marco Polo Airport, a major international hub, lies approximately 100 kilometers from Vicenza. It offers a wider range of flight options, making it a convenient choice for travelers arriving from further afield. Trains connect Venice to Vicenza frequently, with a journey time of around 45 minutes. The bus journey from Venice takes about an hour and a half.

Treviso Airport (TSF): Treviso Airport, a smaller airport north of Venice, serves low-cost airlines and can be a budget-friendly option for reaching Vicenza. However, keep in mind that onward transportation options may be less frequent compared to Verona or Venice. Buses connect Treviso to Vicenza, with a journey time of approximately two hours.

Things to Consider When Flying:

Flight options: Compare flight prices and schedules from various airlines to find the most convenient and budget-friendly option.

Airport transfers: Pre-book your airport transfer from Verona or Venice to Vicenza for a hassle-free arrival.Consider train tickets in advance, or explore shuttle services offered by some hotels.

Luggage: Be mindful of airline baggage restrictions, especially if traveling with budget carriers that often have stricter weight limits.

Taking the Train: A Scenic Journey

Italy boasts an efficient and well-connected railway network, making train travel a popular way to reach Vicenza. Several high-speed trains (Frecciarossa and Italo) and regional trains connect Vicenza to major Italian cities like Milan, Rome,Florence, and Bologna.

Advantages: Train travel offers a comfortable and scenic way to arrive in Vicenza. Many train stations are located in city centers, eliminating the need for further transportation upon arrival.

Disadvantages: Train travel can sometimes be more expensive than flying, particularly for longer journeys. Be sure to book tickets in advance, especially during peak seasons, to secure the best fares.

Planning Your Train Journey:

Websites: Use websites like Trenitalia (https://www.trenitalia.com/en.html) or Omio (https://www.omio.com/) to compare ticket prices and schedules.

Ticket types: Choose between high-speed trains for faster journeys or regional trains for a more budget-friendly option.

Advance booking: Consider booking tickets in advance, especially during peak seasons or for popular connections.

Hitting the Road: Arriving by Car

For those seeking the freedom and flexibility of a road trip, reaching Vicenza by car is a viable option. The A4 motorway (Autostrada A4) serves as the main artery connecting Vicenza to major Italian cities like Milan, Venice, and Padua.

Advantages: Driving allows for a more independent travel experience, letting you stop at charming towns and explore the Italian countryside at your own pace. If traveling with a group, car rentals can be a cost-effective option.

Disadvantages: Driving in Italy can be challenging, especially in cities like Vicenza with limited parking options.Toll roads (autostrade) can add to the cost of a car trip. Be sure to familiarize yourself with Italian traffic regulations before hitting the road.

Things to Consider When Arriving by Car:

International Driving Permit (IDP): Non-EU residents need an International Driving Permit along with their valid driver's license to drive in Italy.

Car rental: Compare car rental options and insurance coverage before booking.

Parking: Parking in city centers like Vicenza can be limited and expensive. Consider using public transportation or parking garages once you arrive.

Beyond Arrival: Getting Around Vicenza

Once you've reached Vicenza, exploring the city and its surrounding areas is easy with various transportation options available.

Walking: The historic center of Vicenza is best explored on foot, allowing you to truly immerse yourself in the city's atmosphere and discover hidden gems tucked away in narrow streets. Many of the city's main attractions are located within walking distance of each other.

Biking: Vicenza offers a bike-sharing program, making it a convenient and eco-friendly way to explore the city.Dedicated bike lanes provide a safe way to navigate the streets.

Public transportation: Vicenza has a well-developed network of buses that connect different parts of the city.Purchasing a daily or multi-day pass can be a cost-effective way to get around.

Taxi: Taxis are readily available in major squares and can be hailed on the street or pre-booked. However, taxis can be a more expensive option compared to public transportation.

Day Trips: For exploring the surrounding region, consider renting a car or participating in organized day trips offered by travel agencies. This allows you to visit charming towns like Verona, Padua, and the rolling hills of the wine country without the hassle of navigation.

Choosing the Right Transportation Option:

The best way to reach and explore Vicenza depends on your travel style, budget, and itinerary.

For a quick and convenient arrival: Consider flying into Verona Airport and taking a short train ride to Vicenza.This is a good option for those on a tight schedule.

For a scenic and comfortable journey: Train travel can be a relaxing and enjoyable way to reach Vicenza,especially for longer journeys from major Italian cities.

For a flexible and independent adventure: Renting a car offers the freedom to explore Vicenza and the surrounding region at your own pace. This option is ideal for those who enjoy road trips and exploring hidden gems off the beaten path.

For a budget-friendly option: Consider taking advantage of public transportation within Vicenza. Walking is also a great way to experience the city and its charming atmosphere.

Vicenza awaits to be discovered, and with its diverse transportation options, getting there and exploring its treasures is an adventure in itself. So, choose your travel style, pack your bags, and embark on a journey to this captivating city in the heart of northern Italy.

Getting around Vicenza - Walking, biking, and public transportation

Vicenza, a treasure trove of Renaissance architecture and rich history, welcomes visitors to wander its charming streets and unveil its hidden gems. But navigating a new city can be daunting. This chapter delves into the convenient and budget-friendly transportation options available within Vicenza, allowing you to explore at your own pace and truly immerse yourself in the city's vibrant energy.

Unveiling Vicenza on Foot:

Vicenza's historic center is a pedestrian paradise, best explored on foot. The compact layout allows you to easily navigate between iconic landmarks like the Basilica Palladiana, the Piazza dei Signori, and the Teatro Olimpico. Here's why walking is the perfect way to experience Vicenza:

Discover hidden gems: Wandering through narrow streets reveals charming squares, tucked-away cafes, and unique shops that buses and cars simply can't access. Walking allows you to stumble upon unexpected delights and get a true sense of the city's atmosphere.

Immerse yourself in the details: Walking allows you to appreciate the intricate architectural details of Palladian palaces, admire the craftsmanship of historic buildings, and soak up the vibrant street life. You might even catch a glimpse of locals chatting at a cafe or children playing in a hidden piazza.

Enjoy the fresh air and sunshine: Vicenza is a walkable city, with most attractions within comfortable walking distance of each other. Strolling through the city allows you to enjoy the fresh air and sunshine, making your exploration a healthy and enjoyable experience.

Budget-friendly option: Walking is completely free, making it the most budget-friendly way to explore Vicenza.For those traveling on a tight budget, walking opens up a world of possibilities without breaking the bank.

Tips for Walking in Vicenza:

Comfortable shoes: Wear comfortable walking shoes as you'll likely spend a good amount of time on your feet exploring the city. Cobblestone streets can be uneven, so choose shoes with good traction.

City map: A good city map or a navigation app can help you find your way around and locate specific landmarks.

Water bottle: Stay hydrated, especially during the warmer months. There are numerous fountains scattered throughout the city where you can refill your water bottle.

Respectful exploration: Be mindful of pedestrians and cyclists as you navigate the streets. Observe local traffic rules and crosswalks for a safe and enjoyable experience.

Biking Through Vicenza:

For those seeking a more active way to explore Vicenza, consider hopping on a bike. The city offers a convenient bike-sharing program, "VicenzaByBike," with several docking stations located throughout the city center.

Benefits of Biking:

Faster than walking: Biking allows you to cover more ground compared to walking, allowing you to explore a wider area of the city within a shorter timeframe.

Fun and healthy: Cycling is a fun and healthy way to explore the city. It provides a bit of exercise while allowing you to enjoy the fresh air and sunshine.

Eco-friendly option: Biking is an environmentally friendly way to get around, minimizing your carbon footprint while exploring the city.

Things to Consider:

Bike-sharing program: The VicenzaByBike program requires registration and charges a nominal fee.Download the app and follow the instructions to rent a bike.

Cycling lanes: Vicenza has dedicated cycling lanes, making it safer for cyclists to navigate the streets.

Traffic awareness: Be aware of pedestrians and other vehicles while cycling. Respect traffic rules and signage for a safe journey.

Helmet: While not mandatory, wearing a helmet is recommended for your safety.

Exploring the City by Bus:

For longer distances or to reach areas outside the city center, Vicenza's well-developed public bus system provides a reliable and convenient option.

Network and Routes: The bus network operates throughout the city, connecting major landmarks, residential areas, and outlying suburbs. Bus routes are clearly displayed at bus stops, and maps are available online or at the tourist information center.

Ticketing: Tickets can be purchased at newsstands ("edicola") or tobacco shops ("tabacchi") displaying the "ATV" (Azienda Trasporti Vicentini) logo. Validate your ticket upon boarding the bus. Consider purchasing a daily or multi-day pass for unlimited travel during the validity period.

Accessibility: Many buses are equipped with ramps or kneeling mechanisms, making them accessible to passengers with disabilities.

Tips for Using Public Buses:

Plan your trip: Download the "SiMobil" app or visit the ATV website (https://www.svt.vi.it/) to plan your journey and find the most convenient bus route.

Bus stops: Identify your nearest bus stop and look for the route number and direction displayed. Wait at the designated stop for the arriving bus.

Onboard communication: Press the stop request button well in advance of your desired stop. Announcements may be made in Italian, but following the visual display on the bus can help you track your location.

Etiquette: Be mindful of other passengers. Allow exiting passengers to disembark before boarding. If the bus is crowded, consider offering your seat to those in need, particularly elderly passengers or individuals with young children. Maintain a respectful noise level to ensure a comfortable journey for everyone.

Beyond the City Center:

While walking, biking, and public buses are excellent options for exploring Vicenza's core, venturing beyond the historic center opens doors to new discoveries.

Day Trips by Bus: The Vicenza bus network extends to surrounding towns and villages, allowing you to explore the Palladian villas scattered across the countryside or visit charming towns like Bassano del Grappa or

Marostica.These day trips offer a glimpse into the rich history and diverse landscapes of the Veneto region.

Organized Tours: Several travel agencies offer day tours from Vicenza, often including transportation, guided visits, and entrance fees. This option is convenient for those seeking a hassle-free experience and insights from local experts.

Choosing the Right Option:

The best way to get around Vicenza depends on your needs and preferences:

For a personal and immersive experience: Walking is the ideal way to explore the historic center, allowing you to truly connect with the city's atmosphere and discover hidden gems.

For a faster pace and wider exploration: Cycling allows you to cover more ground and explore areas slightly further from the city center. It's a fun and healthy option for active travelers.

For longer distances and accessibility: The public bus system offers a reliable and affordable way to reach various parts of the city and explore surrounding areas.

A City for Every Explorer:

Vicenza's diverse transportation options cater to various travel styles and budgets. Whether you choose to explore on foot,navigate the city by bike, or hop on a public bus, getting around Vicenza is a breeze. So, lace up your walking shoes, grab a bike, or plan your bus route, and embark on an unforgettable journey through this captivating Italian city. With its charming streets, historical landmarks, and vibrant atmosphere, Vicenza awaits you with open arms!

Chapter two

Vicenza, a jewel nestled amidst the rolling hills of Italy's Veneto region, beckons travelers with its rich history,architectural splendor, and vibrant culture. But before embarking on your Italian adventure, meticulous planning ensures a smooth and unforgettable experience. This chapter serves as your comprehensive guide, outlining everything you need to consider when planning your trip to Vicenza.

Deciding When to Visit:

Vicenza's charm unfolds throughout the year, each season offering a unique experience. Here's a breakdown to help you choose the perfect time for your visit:

Spring (March-May): A season of awakening, spring paints Vicenza in vibrant hues. Pleasant weather allows for comfortable exploration, while fewer crowds enhance the tranquility. Witness blooming landscapes and participate in outdoor events like music concerts or traditional festivals.

Summer (June-August): The city transforms into a vibrant hub, bustling with festivals, open-air performances,and street markets. Long sunny days are ideal for exploring the city and surrounding countryside. However, expect higher temperatures and larger crowds. Don't forget your sunglasses and sunscreen!

Fall (September-November): As summer fades, Vicenza embraces a season of tranquility. Comfortable temperatures and reduced crowds create a perfect atmosphere for exploring at your own pace. Immerse yourself in the harvest celebrations and capture the breathtaking autumn colors with your camera.

Winter (December-February): The city transforms into a magical wonderland with Christmas markets offering festive cheer. Lower accommodation rates make winter a budget-friendly option. Explore museums and art galleries to escape the winter chill, or enjoy cozy evenings indulging in hearty Vicentine cuisine.

Accommodation Options:

From charming boutique hotels to historic palazzos, Vicenza offers a diverse range of accommodation options to suit every budget and preference. Here's what to consider when choosing your stay:

Location: Decide whether you want to be nestled in the heart of the historic center or prefer a quieter area outside the city walls. The city center offers convenient access to major attractions, while staying outside may provide a more peaceful atmosphere and budget-friendly options.

Hotel amenities: Consider the amenities that are important to you, such as breakfast included, fitness centers, spas,or parking facilities. Boutique hotels might offer a more personalized experience, while larger chain hotels often provide standardized amenities.

Budget: Vicenza caters to various budgets. Luxury hotels offer opulent experiences, while budget-friendly hostels and guesthouses provide basic amenities at a lower cost. Consider your needs and prioritize the features you value most.

Tips for Booking Accommodation:

Research and compare: Utilize online travel booking platforms or hotel websites to compare prices and amenities.Read reviews by previous guests to gain insights into the property and its atmosphere.

Book in advance: Especially during peak seasons, booking your accommodation well in advance is crucial to secure your preferred option and avoid disappointment.

Consider special offers: Many hotels offer seasonal discounts or packages that may include breakfast or airport transfers. Look out for these deals to save money on your stay.

Visas and Immigration:

Citizens of most European Union (EU) countries do not require a visa to visit Italy for stays less than 90 days. However,non-EU citizens may need to obtain a Schengen visa depending on their nationality and the duration of their stay.

Check Visa Requirements: Before booking your trip, research visa requirements for Italy specific to your nationality. Government websites or embassies can provide the necessary information.

Application Process: If required, initiate the visa application process well in advance of your trip. Gather the necessary documents and ensure you meet all eligibility criteria.

Essential Travel Documents:

Ensure you have all the essential travel documents in order for a smooth immigration process:

Valid Passport: Your passport must be valid for at least six months beyond your intended departure date from Italy.

Visa (if applicable): If required, ensure you have obtained the appropriate Schengen visa for your stay.

Travel Insurance: Consider purchasing comprehensive travel insurance to cover potential medical emergencies,trip cancellations, or lost luggage.

Currency Exchange:

The official currency in Italy is the Euro (EUR). Exchange your home currency for Euros before your trip or use ATMs upon arrival. Be aware of exchange rates and fees associated with currency exchange services.

Planning Your Activities:

Vicenza offers a plethora of activities, from exploring museums and historical sites to attending festivals and indulging in culinary delights.

Research attractions: Research online resources, travel blogs, or guidebooks to create a list of activities that align with your interests. Consider museums you'd like to visit

Consider museums you'd like to visit: Explore the vast collections at the Basilica Palladiana or learn about the city's history at the Museo Civico di Palazzo Chiericati. Check opening hours and consider purchasing tickets in advance, especially during peak season, to avoid long queues.

Plan for events: Vicenza hosts a vibrant calendar of events throughout the year. Research upcoming festivals,concerts, or theatrical performances that coincide with your visit. Participating in local events allows you to immerse yourself in the city's culture and connect with the community.

Explore the culinary scene: Vicenza is a haven for food lovers. Plan your meals around traditional dishes like "risotto al Baccalà" (cod risotto) or "bigoli con l'anatra" (thick spaghetti with duck sauce). Discover local delicacies at bustling street markets or indulge in a multi-course meal at a historic restaurant.

Day trips from Vicenza: Venture beyond the city limits and explore the surrounding region. The Veneto is dotted with charming towns like Bassano del Grappa, famous for its grappa distilleries, or Marostica, known for its living chess game played every two years. Several Palladian villas, architectural masterpieces by Andrea Palladio, are scattered across the countryside, offering a glimpse into Renaissance-era artistry. Consider day trips by bus or join organized tours for a hassle-free experience.

Transportation Options:

Getting around Vicenza is a breeze with various transportation options available:

Walking: The historic center of Vicenza is best explored on foot. Stroll through charming piazzas, admire architectural details, and soak up the city's atmosphere at your own pace. Walking maps are readily available at tourist information centers.

Cycling: Rent a bike for a fun and healthy way to explore the city and its surroundings. Dedicated bike lanes offer a safe environment for cyclists. Consider cycling to nearby Palladian villas for a scenic adventure.

Public Buses: The city's efficient bus network provides a reliable and affordable way to reach various parts of Vicenza and explore outlying areas. Purchase tickets in advance from newsstands or authorized vendors.

Useful Resources:

Tourist Information Center: Visit the Vicenza Tourist Information Center to obtain maps, brochures, and recommendations for attractions, restaurants, and events. Ask friendly staff for personalized advice to plan your itinerary.

Travel Apps: Download travel apps like Google Maps or Citymapper to navigate the city efficiently. These apps offer public transportation routes, walking directions, and real-time updates.

Travel Guides: Invest in a good travel guide or utilize online resources to learn about Vicenza's history, culture,and must-see attractions. These guides provide valuable insights and recommendations to enhance your experience.

Packing Essentials:

Pack strategically to ensure you have everything you need for a comfortable and enjoyable trip:

Clothing: Adapt your clothing choices to the season. During summer, pack lightweight, breathable clothing,sunglasses, and a hat. For winter, pack warm layers, waterproof shoes, and a scarf. No matter the season,comfortable walking shoes are essential.

Essentials: Don't forget essential items like a reusable water bottle, sunscreen, a camera, and a power adapter if needed. A basic first-aid kit is also recommended.

Travel documents: Keep your passport, visa (if applicable), travel insurance details, and booking confirmations readily accessible in a secure location.

Learning a Few Italian Phrases:

While English is understood in some tourist areas, learning a few basic Italian phrases can enhance your experience:

- **Buongiorno/Buonasera (Good morning/Good evening):** A polite greeting.
- **Grazie (Thank you):** Express your gratitude.
- **Scusi (Excuse me):** A way to politely get someone's attention.
- **Mi scusi, non parlo italiano (Excuse me, I don't speak Italian):** If you need assistance.

Embracing the Local Culture:

Respect the local culture and traditions to make a positive impression on the community. Dress modestly when visiting religious sites. Be mindful of noise levels in public spaces. Learn a few basic Italian phrases to show your interest in the local culture.

By following these tips and planning your itinerary thoughtfully, you can ensure your trip to Vicenza is an unforgettable adventure filled with cultural immersion, historical exploration, and delicious culinary experiences. So, pack your bags,unleash your wanderlust, and get ready to discover the magic of Vicenza!

Budgeting for your Vicenza adventure - Accommodation options for all budgets

Vicenza, a treasure trove of Renaissance architecture and rich history, welcomes visitors from all walks of life. But navigating the costs associated with travel can be daunting. This chapter delves into budgeting strategies and explores a range of accommodation options in Vicenza, ensuring an unforgettable experience without breaking the bank.

Planning Your Budget:

Before embarking on your Vicentine adventure, establish a realistic budget that encompasses all your travel expenses.Consider the following factors:

Transportation: Factor in the cost of flights or train tickets, airport transfers, and your chosen mode of transportation within the city (walking, cycling, or public buses).

Accommodation: Research and compare accommodation options based on your budget and preferences.

Activities: List the attractions you'd like to visit and factor in entrance fees, tours, or event tickets.

Food: Decide whether you'll primarily dine at restaurants, explore local markets for self-catering, or opt for a combination of both. Research average meal prices to estimate your food budget.

Additional Expenses: Include spending money for souvenirs, drinks, unexpected costs, and travel insurance (recommended).

Accommodation Strategies:

Accommodation is often a significant expense when traveling. Here's a breakdown of various options in Vicenza to suit your budget:

Budget-Friendly Options:

Hostels: Hostels offer dorm beds, a social atmosphere, and basic amenities at the most affordable price point. They are ideal for solo travelers or those seeking a budget-conscious experience. Hostels in Vicenza typically range from €20-€40 per night for a bed in a shared dorm room.

Budget Hotels: Several budget-friendly hotels offer clean, comfortable rooms with basic amenities like Wi-Fi and breakfast (sometimes included). These hotels are a good choice for those who prioritize convenience and a private space without extravagant amenities. Budget hotels in Vicenza range from €50-€80 per night for a standard double room.

Mid-Range Options:

B&Bs (Bed and Breakfasts): B&Bs offer a charming and personalized experience. They are often housed in historic buildings and provide comfortable rooms with breakfast included. This option allows you to interact with local hosts and gain insights into the city's culture. B&Bs in Vicenza typically range from €80-€120 per night for a double room.

Boutique Hotels: Vicenza boasts a collection of charming boutique hotels housed in renovated palazzos or modern buildings. These hotels offer a unique ambiance, personalized service, and often include amenities like rooftop terraces or spa facilities. Boutique hotels in Vicenza range from €120-€200 per night for a double room.

Luxury Options:

Luxury Hotels: For those seeking an opulent experience, Vicenza offers a selection of luxury hotels renowned for their impeccable service, elegant décor, and high-end amenities like spa treatments, fitness centers, and fine-dining restaurants. Luxury hotels in Vicenza start from €200 per night for a double room and can reach significantly higher prices depending on the specific hotel and season.

Alternative Options:

Apartments: Renting an apartment allows for a more independent and homey experience, especially for longer stays. Apartments offer kitchen facilities, providing the flexibility to cook some meals and save on dining costs.Online platforms like Airbnb or Booking.com list apartment rentals in Vicenza. Prices vary depending on location,size, and amenities, but generally start from €80 per night for a studio apartment.

Agriturismos: Escape the city center and experience rural life by staying at an agriturismo. These farm stays offer comfortable accommodations, often with breakfast included, and the chance to immerse yourself in the local agricultural way of life. Agriturismos can be a unique and budget-friendly option for those seeking a countryside experience. Prices vary depending on the location and amenities, but generally start from €70 per night for a double room.

Tips for Finding Affordable Accommodation:

Book in advance: Especially during peak seasons, booking your accommodation well in advance secures the best deals and avoids disappointment regarding availability.

Consider location: Staying outside the historic center can be significantly cheaper. Vicenza is a walkable city, so consider a slightly further location if you prioritize budget over central convenience.

Compare prices: Utilize online travel booking platforms or hotel websites to compare prices and amenities across different options.

Look for discounts: Many hotels offer seasonal discounts or packages that might include breakfast or airport transfers. Consider these deals to save money on your stay.

shoulder seasons (spring and fall) can offer significant savings on accommodation compared to peak summer months. The weather during these seasons is often pleasant, with fewer crowds allowing for a more relaxed exploration of the city.

Additional Savings:

Beyond accommodation, here are some additional tips to save money on your Vicenza adventure:

Free Activities: Vicenza boasts a plethora of free activities. Wander through the charming piazzas, explore the Basilica Palladiana's exterior, or admire the architectural marvels lining the streets. Many museums offer free entry on specific days, so research beforehand and plan your visits accordingly.

Self-Catering: While indulging in Vicentine cuisine is a must, consider incorporating self-catering options for some meals. Stock up on fresh produce and local delicacies at the vibrant markets like the "Mercato delle Erbe" (Herb Market).

Public Transportation: Walking is the best way to explore the historic center, but for longer distances, utilize the efficient public bus system. Purchase daily or multi-day passes for unlimited travel during the validity period to save on individual tickets.

Picnics in the Park: Pack a picnic lunch with fresh bread, cheese, and local specialties purchased at the market.Enjoy a leisurely lunch break in the beautiful Giardino Salvi, surrounded by nature and historical landmarks.

Travel During the Week: Flight and accommodation prices often drop during weekdays compared to weekends.Consider traveling during the week to potentially save money on transportation and lodging.

Finding the Perfect Fit:

The ideal accommodation in Vicenza depends on your budget, travel style, and priorities.

For solo travelers or budget-conscious explorers: Hostels or budget hotels offer a comfortable and affordable base for exploring the city.

For those seeking a personalized experience: B&Bs provide a charming atmosphere and the opportunity to connect with local hosts.

For travelers seeking unique experiences: Consider boutique hotels or agriturismos for a touch of luxury or a rural escape.

For those prioritizing luxury and high-end amenities: Opulent hotels in Vicenza cater to those seeking an unforgettable stay in a sophisticated setting.

Visas and currency exchange - Essential information for international travelers

Vicenza, a captivating city steeped in Renaissance history and vibrant culture, beckons international travelers with its architectural marvels, delectable cuisine, and captivating festivals. But before embarking on your Italian adventure,ensuring you have the necessary travel documents and understanding currency exchange procedures is crucial. This chapter equips you with essential information for a smooth and hassle-free arrival in Vicenza.

Visa Requirements

Understanding the Schengen Zone:

Italy is part of the Schengen Zone, a group of 26 European countries that allow passport holders of member nations to travel freely within the zone without border controls. If you are a citizen of a Schengen member country, you generally do not require a visa for stays in Italy less than 90 days.

Visa Requirements for Non-Schengen Zone Citizens:

Citizens of countries outside the Schengen Zone may require a visa to enter Italy, depending on their nationality and the duration of their stay. Here's how to determine if you need a visa:

Visa Checker: Utilize the Italian Ministry of Foreign Affairs' visa checker tool (https://www.esteri.it/en/) to determine if your nationality requires a visa.

Embassy or Consulate: Contact the nearest Italian embassy or consulate in your home country. They provide accurate and up-to-date information on visa requirements, application procedures, and necessary documents.

Types of Visas for Italy:

The type of visa you need depends on the purpose and duration of your visit. Here are the most common types of visas for visiting Italy:

Schengen Tourist Visa (C Visa): This short-stay visa allows tourist visits for up to 90 days within a 180-day period. It is the most common visa for visiting Vicenza.

Long-Stay Visa (D Visa): This visa is required for stays exceeding 90 days, such as studying, working, or volunteering in Italy.

Applying for a Visa:

If required, applying for a visa typically involves the following steps:

Gather Documents: Compile the required documents as instructed by the Italian embassy or consulate. These may include your passport, visa application form, proof of travel insurance, accommodation bookings, and financial resources to support your stay.

Schedule an Appointment: Contact the Italian embassy or consulate to schedule an appointment for visa application submission.

Application Fees: Be prepared to pay the visa application fee, which varies depending on your nationality and visa type. Payment methods may differ, so confirm with the embassy or consulate beforehand.

Processing Time: Allow sufficient time for visa processing, typically ranging from a few days to several weeks.

Important Tips for Visa Application:

Apply Early: Initiate the visa application process well in advance of your trip, especially during peak seasons.

Complete Applications: Ensure your application is complete and all required documents are submitted to avoid delays or rejections.

Double-Check Requirements: Carefully review visa requirements and application procedures to ensure you comply with all regulations.

Currency Exchange and Payment Options in Vicenza

The Official Currency:

Italy, including Vicenza, uses the Euro (EUR) as its official currency. Plan to exchange your home currency for Euros before your trip or utilize ATMs upon arrival. Here's a breakdown of currency exchange options:

Exchanging Currency Before Your Trip: Exchange some of your home currency for Euros at banks or currency exchange bureaus in your home country. This provides you with cash for immediate expenses upon arrival in Vicenza.

ATMs: ATMs are widely available throughout Vicenza, allowing you to withdraw Euros using your international debit or credit card. Be aware of potential ATM fees charged by your bank and the ATM operator.

Travel Cards: Consider pre-paid travel cards loaded with Euros. These cards can be used for ATM withdrawals and payments at participating merchants.

Using Credit and Debit Cards:

Major credit cards like Visa, Mastercard, and American Express are widely accepted in Vicenza, particularly at hotels,restaurants, and larger shops. However, smaller shops and local markets might primarily accept cash. Inform your bank about your travel plans to avoid card blockage due to suspicious activity in a new location.

Travel Tips for Managing Money:

Carry a Mix of Cash and Cards: Having a mix of cash and credit/debit cards allows flexibility for various situations.

Notify Your Bank: Inform your bank about your travel dates and destination to avoid card blockage due to suspected fraudulent activity.

Set Spending Limits: Consider setting spending limits on your credit card to manage your travel budget effectively.

Beware of Currency Exchange Scams: Be cautious of street vendors offering significantly lower exchange rates.Utilize reputable exchange bureaus or banks for secure transactions.

Compare ATM Fees: Before using an ATM, check the withdrawal fees associated with your bank and the ATM operator. Consider using ATMs affiliated with your bank for potentially lower fees.

Additional Payment Options:

Mobile Wallets: Apple Pay, Google Pay, and other mobile wallet services are gaining popularity in Italy. If your phone supports these options and the merchant has contactless payment terminals, you can utilize them for convenient and secure transactions.

Prepaid Cards: Prepaid travel cards loaded with Euros can be a safe and convenient way to manage your spending.These cards can be used for ATM withdrawals and payments at participating merchants.

Understanding Costs in Vicenza:

While Vicenza is generally cheaper than major Italian cities like Rome or Milan, budgeting for your trip is essential.Here's a breakdown of some average costs to consider:

Accommodation: Prices vary significantly depending on location, room type, and season. Expect budget hotels to start around €50 per night, while luxury hotels can reach significantly higher prices.

Food: Enjoying a sit-down meal at a restaurant can range from €20-€50 per person, while grabbing a quick bite at a cafe or market stall can be much cheaper.

Activities: Entrance fees for museums and attractions can range from €5-€20. Public transportation passes offer cost-effective travel options.

Souvenirs: Prices for souvenirs can vary widely depending on the type and quality. Haggling is sometimes acceptable at street markets.

Saving Money in Vicenza:

Embrace the local culture and explore budget-friendly options to stretch your travel budget:

Free Activities: Vicenza boasts numerous free activities, from exploring the charming piazzas to attending open-air concerts in the summer.

Self-Catering: Stock up on fresh produce and local delicacies from vibrant markets like the "Mercato delle Erbe" (Herb Market). Enjoy picnics in beautiful parks or cook meals in your accommodation if you have kitchen facilities.

Public Transportation: Walking is the best way to explore the historic center, but for longer distances, utilize the efficient and affordable public bus system.

Travel During Off-Peak Seasons: Consider traveling during the shoulder seasons (spring and fall) when accommodation and flight prices are typically lower compared to peak summer months.

Packing essentials - What to bring for your Vicenza trip

Vicenza, a treasure trove of Renaissance architecture and vibrant culture, beckons travelers with its captivating charm. To ensure a smooth and enjoyable experience, packing strategically is crucial. This chapter serves as your comprehensive guide to essential items for your Vicenza adventure, taking into account the season, local customs, and activities you plan.

Planning Your Packing List:

Before diving into specific items, consider the following factors to tailor your packing list:

Season: Vicenza experiences distinct seasonal variations. Pack lightweight, breathable clothing for summer (June-August), comfortable layers for spring and fall (March-May & September-November), and warm clothes,waterproof shoes, and a scarf for winter (December-February).

Activities: Plan your outfits based on your itinerary. If you plan on visiting religious sites, pack modest clothing.For outdoor activities, pack comfortable walking shoes and weather-appropriate clothing. Consider bringing a swimsuit if you plan to visit thermal baths or enjoy a refreshing dip in a lake near Vicenza.

Travel Style: Are you a budget backpacker, a comfort-seeker prioritizing convenience, or a fashion enthusiast wanting to dress to impress? Packing reflects your travel style, so choose outfits that make you feel confident and comfortable throughout your trip.

Essential Clothing:

Tops: Pack a mix of versatile tops like t-shirts, blouses, or light sweaters (depending on the season). Consider bringing a long-sleeved shirt for layering and evenings, even in summer.

Bottoms: Pack comfortable walking shoes for exploring the city. Jeans, lightweight trousers, or breathable skirts are practical options. Include a dressier pair of pants or a skirt for evenings out if desired.

Underwear: Pack enough comfortable underwear for the duration of your trip.

Socks: Bring a mix of breathable socks for walking and warmer socks for cooler weather.

Outerwear: Depending on the season, pack a light jacket, raincoat, or a warm coat. Scarves and hats can be additional essentials for cooler weather.

Additional Clothing Considerations:

Pajamas: Pack comfortable sleepwear for a good night's rest.

Swimsuit: Consider packing a swimsuit if you plan on visiting thermal baths or enjoying a refreshing dip in a lake near Vicenza.

Undergarments: Pack a comfortable sports bra for active pursuits, especially if you plan on hiking or biking.

Dress Code: If you plan on visiting religious sites like the Duomo (cathedral), pack clothing that covers your shoulders and knees. A scarf can be a handy solution to cover bare arms or legs when needed.

Footwear:

Walking Shoes: Comfortable walking shoes are essential for exploring Vicenza's charming streets. Prioritize shoes with good traction to navigate cobblestone streets.

Additional Shoes: Consider packing a comfortable pair of sandals for warm weather or dressier shoes for evenings out, depending on your preferences.

Accessories:

Sunglasses: Protect your eyes from the Italian sun with a stylish pair of sunglasses.

Hat: Pack a hat to shield yourself from the sun, especially during the summer months. Choose a hat with a wide brim for optimal sun protection.

Scarf: A versatile scarf can be used for warmth, to cover your shoulders when visiting religious sites, or as a stylish accessory.

Belt: A belt can be a helpful accessory to adjust the fit of your clothing.

Essentials for All Seasons:

Underwear: Comfortable undergarments are vital for any season.

Pajamas: Pack comfortable sleepwear for a good night's rest.

Toiletries: Pack your essential toiletries like shampoo, conditioner, soap, toothpaste, toothbrush, and any medications you require. Consider travel-sized versions for convenience and space-saving. Sunscreen and insect repellent are crucial during summer months.

Electronics: Pack your phone charger, a portable battery pack if needed, and any device adapters required for Italian power outlets. Download essential travel apps like Google Maps or Citymapper for navigation.

Travel Documents:

Passport: Ensure your passport is valid for at least six months beyond your intended departure date from Italy.

Visa (if applicable): If required, obtain the appropriate Schengen visa for your stay in Italy.

Travel Insurance: Consider purchasing comprehensive travel insurance to cover potential medical emergencies,trip cancellations, or lost luggage.

Booking Confirmations: Retain digital or printed copies of your accommodation and activity bookings for easy reference.

Additional Considerations:

Water Bottle: Pack a reusable water bottle to stay hydrated while exploring the city. Vicenza boasts numerous public fountains where you can refill your bottle, saving money and reducing plastic waste.

First-Aid Kit: Pack a basic first-aid kit containing essential items like bandages, antiseptic wipes, pain relievers,and any medications you might need.

Snacks: Having a few snacks on hand can be helpful for unexpected delays or hunger pangs between meals. Pack energy bars, nuts, or dried fruit for convenient and healthy options.

Laundry Detergent: Consider packing a small amount of travel-sized laundry detergent if you plan on doing laundry during your stay, especially for longer trips.

Entertainment: Pack a book, journal, or download movies or music on your device for entertainment during downtime or travel. Learning a few basic Italian phrases can enhance your experience and impress locals.

Small Umbrella: A compact, foldable umbrella can be a lifesaver if you encounter sudden showers, particularly during spring and fall.

Lock: Consider packing a small lock for added security, especially if you're staying in hostels or dorm rooms.

Packing Smart:

Maximize Space: Utilize packing cubes or space-saving techniques like rolling clothes to maximize space in your luggage. Choose versatile clothing items that can be mixed and matched to create multiple outfits.

Check Airline Restrictions: Before packing, familiarize yourself with your airline's baggage allowance for checked and carry-on luggage. Pay attention to weight and size restrictions to avoid additional charges at the airport.

Label Your Luggage: Clearly label your luggage with your name, contact information, and destination to avoid any confusion or mishaps.

Embrace the Local Culture:

While packing, consider these tips to seamlessly integrate into the local culture:

Dress modestly: When visiting religious sites, pack clothing that covers your shoulders and knees. A scarf is a handy solution for quick adjustments.

Pack light: Vicenza is a walkable city, so avoid overpacking heavy luggage that can be cumbersome while navigating cobblestone streets.

Be Eco-conscious: Pack a reusable water bottle and shopping bags to minimize waste. Consider bringing a light scarf instead of bulky towels for thermal baths, as some facilities might provide them.

Staying connected - Internet access and phone options

Vicenza, a captivating city steeped in Renaissance charm, beckons travelers from around the world. But staying connected with loved ones back home and accessing the internet for navigation, research, and social media sharing is crucial during your trip. This chapter equips you with essential information on internet access and phone options in Vicenza, ensuring you stay connected throughout your Italian adventure.

Mobile Phone Options:

There are three main ways to use your phone for calls, texts, and internet access in Vicenza:

Using Your Existing Phone Plan (Roaming):

Contact Your Provider: Before your trip, contact your mobile phone provider to inquire about international roaming charges in Italy. Roaming charges can be exorbitant, so understanding the costs involved is crucial.

Consider Roaming Packages: Many mobile providers offer temporary roaming packages that allow a specific data allowance and call minutes for a fixed price during your travel period. Compare plans and choose the one that best suits your usage needs.

Beware of Hidden Fees: Be mindful of potential hidden fees associated with roaming, such as data overage charges or receiving calls. Consider setting data usage alerts to avoid exceeding your plan limits.

Purchasing a Local SIM Card:

Benefits: Purchasing a local SIM card is often the most affordable option for internet access and calls within Italy.Local SIM cards provide Italian phone numbers, allowing you to receive calls and texts at a flat rate.

Where to Buy: Local SIM cards are readily available at airports, phone company stores like TIM, Vodafone, and Wind, and newsstands throughout Vicenza.

Choose a Plan: Mobile providers offer a variety of prepaid SIM card plans with varying data allowances, call minutes, and validity periods. Choose a plan that aligns with your anticipated usage.

Activation: The SIM card activation process is usually straightforward. Store staff can assist you with activation,which might involve showing your passport and providing a top-up for your chosen plan.

Renting a Portable Wi-Fi Device:

Convenience: Renting a portable Wi-Fi device (also known as a MiFi) offers a convenient way to connect multiple devices (phone, laptop, tablet) to the internet simultaneously. This option is ideal if you're traveling with a group or require a reliable internet connection for work.

Rental Companies: Numerous online companies offer portable Wi-Fi rentals for travelers. Pick-up and drop-off locations are available at airports or convenient locations within the city.

Costs: Rental fees vary depending on the rental duration, data allowance, and device capabilities. Compare prices and features before booking.

Data Usage: Be mindful of data usage limitations associated with rented Wi-Fi devices. Exceeding data limits can incur additional charges.

Finding Free Wi-Fi:

While not the most reliable option, free Wi-Fi hotspots can be found in various locations throughout Vicenza:

Public Squares and Parks: Some central piazzas and public parks offer free Wi-Fi access. Connection speeds and reliability might vary.

Cafes and Restaurants: Many cafes and restaurants offer complimentary Wi-Fi for their customers. Purchase a drink or meal to access the internet while enjoying a relaxing break.

Hotels and Accommodations: Most hotels and accommodations include Wi-Fi access in their room rates.Connection speeds and reliability are typically good within hotel premises.

Important Considerations:

Unlocking Your Phone: Ensure your phone is unlocked to utilize a local SIM card in Italy. Contact your mobile provider to unlock your phone if necessary.

Dual SIM Phones: If you have a dual-SIM phone, you can keep your home SIM card active for receiving calls and texts while using a local SIM card for data and Italian calls.

Learn Basic Italian Phrases: Knowing a few basic Italian phrases like "Posso avere il Wi-Fi per favore?" (Can I have the Wi-Fi please?) can be helpful for inquiring about internet access.

Staying Secure Online:

Public Wi-Fi Risks: Be cautious when using public Wi-Fi networks, as they can be less secure than private networks. Avoid accessing sensitive information like bank accounts or credit card details on public Wi-Fi.

VPN: Consider using a Virtual Private Network (VPN) to encrypt your online activity and add an extra layer of security, especially when using public Wi-Fi.

Making Calls:

Country Code: Italy's country code is +39. To call an Italian number from abroad, dial +39 followed by the local phone number.

Calling Cards: While less common nowadays, purchasing international calling cards can be an option for making calls back home. Compare rates and choose a plan that aligns with your calling needs.

Staying Informed:

Download Apps: Download offline maps and translation apps before your trip. These apps can be invaluable for navigating the city and communicating with locals even without an internet connection.

Local Tourist Information: Pick up free brochures and maps from the Vicenza Tourist Information Office. They often provide information on Wi-Fi hotspots and internet cafes within the city.

Embrace the Experience:

Staying connected with loved ones back home and having access to the internet is essential for many travelers. By understanding your options and choosing the method that best suits your needs and budget, you can ensure seamless communication and access to information during your Vicenza adventure.

Here are some additional tips to maximize your connected experience:

Prioritize Face-to-Face Interaction: While staying connected online is important, don't let it overshadow the joy of exploring Vicenza in person. Embrace the opportunity to interact with locals, learn about their culture, and create lasting memories.

Disconnect to Reconnect: Schedule some time to disconnect from your phone and immerse yourself in the sights and sounds of Vicenza. This allows you to truly appreciate the moment and create a deeper connection with the city.

Capture Memories: Use your phone's camera to capture your Vicenza adventure. Take photos of landmarks,delicious food, and unique experiences. These pictures will be your personal souvenirs to cherish and share long after your trip.

Chapter three

Essential Phrases in Italian - Learning the basics for a smooth trip

Embarking on a trip to Vicenza, Italy, promises an unforgettable experience filled with historical wonders, delectable cuisine, and vibrant culture. However, navigating a new country can be daunting, especially if you don't speak the language. This chapter equips you with essential Italian phrases to enhance your communication and ensure a smooth and enjoyable trip.

The Importance of Learning Basic Italian:

While English is spoken to some degree in tourist areas, learning a few basic Italian phrases demonstrates respect for the local culture and can significantly enhance your experience. It can:

Break the Ice: A simple greeting in Italian can make a positive first impression and encourage friendly interactions with locals.

Navigate with Ease: Asking for directions or understanding basic signs becomes much easier with a few key Italian phrases.

Order Food with Confidence: Communicate your preferences and dietary restrictions more effectively when ordering food at restaurants or cafes.

Enhance the Shopping Experience: Basic Italian allows you to haggle at markets, inquire about products, and understand product descriptions.

Build Rapport: Locals appreciate tourists who attempt to speak their language, fostering a more positive and enriching experience.

Getting Started with Pronunciation:

Italian pronunciation is relatively straightforward, with a few key differences from English. Here's a quick guide:

Vowels: Italian vowels are pronounced clearly and cleanly. "A" is like "ah" in "father," "E" sounds like "eh" in "bed," "I" is like "ee" in "feet," "O" is like "oh" in "hope," and "U" is like "oo" in "boot."

Double Consonants: Double consonants are pronounced as a single, stronger consonant sound. For example,"cappuccino" (kah-poo-chee-no) has a double "p" that creates a stronger "p" sound.

G and H: The letter "G" before "i" or "e" is pronounced like a "j" in English. For example, "gelato" (jeh-LAH-toh) has a soft "g" sound. The letter "H" is generally silent in Italian.

Essential Greetings and Phrases:

Buongiorno/Buonasera: Good morning/Good afternoon/Good evening (used until sunset) - Boo-ohn-JOR-no / Boo-oh-na-SEH-ra

Buona notte: Good night - Boo-oh-na NOHT-teh

Arrivederci: Goodbye (formal) - Ar-ree-vay-DER-chee

Ciao: Hello/Goodbye (informal) - CHOW

Grazie: Thank you - GRAH-tsee-eh

Prego: You're welcome (also used for "please") - PRAY-go

Scusi: Excuse me - SKOO-zee

Mi scusi: Excuse me (more formal) - Mee SKOO-zee

Asking for Help and Directions:

Mi può aiutare? (formal) / Mi aiuti? (informal): Can you help me? - Mee PWO-oo ah-yoo-TARE? / Mee ah-YOU-tee?

Non capisco: I don't understand - Nohn kah-PEE-sko

Dove si trova...? Where is...? - DOH-veh see TRO-va...? (Fill in the blank with the place name)

Come si arriva a...? How do I get to...? - KOH-meh see ar-REE-va ah...? (Fill in the blank with the place name)

Scusi, dov'è il bagno? Excuse me, where is the bathroom? - SKOO-zee, doh-veh eh il BAN-yo?

Ordering Food and Drinks:

Vorrei... per favore: I would like... please - Vohr-RAY... per fah-VOH-reh

Posso avere il menu, per favore? Can I have the menu, please? - Posso ah-VEH-reh il meh-NOO, per fah-VOH-reh?

Posso avere un bicchiere d'acqua, per favore? Can I have a glass of water, please? - Posso ah-VEH-reh oon bee-KYEH-reh dahk-kwa, per fah-VOH-reh?

Ha/hanno (singular/plural) opzioni vegetariane/senza glutine? Do you have vegetarian/gluten-free options? - Ah/AHN-no op- tsee-OH-ni ve-jeh-tah-RYAH-neh / sen-tsa gloo-TEE-neh?

Il conto, per favore: The check, please - Il CON-to, per fah-VOH-reh

Posso pagare con la carta di credito? Can I pay with credit card? - Posso pah-GAH-reh con la CAR-ta dee CRE-dee-toh?

Essential Shopping Phrases:

Quanto costa? How much does it cost? - KWAHN-toh KOH-sta?

Posso provare...? Can I try...? - Posso proh-VAH-reh...? (Fill in the blank with the item)

Vorrei prendere... I would like to take... - Vohr-RAY pren-DEH-reh... (Fill in the blank with the item)

C'è uno sconto? Is there a discount? - Cheh oonoh SKON-to?

Grazie, non prendo altro. Thank you, I don't need anything else. - GRAH-tsee-eh, non pren-do AHL-tro.

Basic Courtesy Phrases:

Mi dispiace: I'm sorry - Mee dee-SPLAH-cheh

Grazie mille: Thank you very much - GRAH-tsee-eh MEE-leh

Non c'è problema: No problem - Nohn cheh proh-BLEH-ma

Buona giornata: Have a good day - Boo-oh-na jor-NAH-ta

Buona fortuna: Good luck - Boo-oh-na for-TOO-na

Numbers:

Understanding basic numbers can be helpful for shopping, public transportation, and understanding time. Here are the numbers 1-10:

- Uno (OON-oh) - One
- Due (DOO-eh) - Two
- Tre (TREH) - Three
- Quattro (KWATT-ro) - Four
- Cinque (CHEEN-kweh) - Five
- Sei (SAY) - Six
- Sette (SET-teh) - Seven
- Otto (OH-toh) - Eight
- Nove (NOH-veh) - Nine
- Dieci (DYE-chi) - Ten

Additional Resources:

Phrasebooks: Invest in a basic Italian phrasebook for quick reference during your trip.

Language Learning Apps: Numerous mobile apps like Duolingo and Memrise offer free or paid options to learn basic Italian vocabulary and phrases.

Online Learning Platforms: Websites like BBC Languages - Italian and Babbel offer online Italian courses for beginners.

Embrace the Learning Experience:

Learning basic Italian phrases doesn't require fluency. Focus on memorizing a few key phrases that you can use confidently throughout your trip. Don't be afraid to make mistakes - Italians appreciate the effort tourists put into learning their language. Learning a few basic phrases can be a fun and rewarding experience that adds a whole new dimension to your Vicenza adventure.

Staying Safe and Healthy - Healthcare information and safety tips

A trip to Vicenza promises a captivating blend of historical landmarks, delectable cuisine, and vibrant culture. While safety is a priority in any travel experience, being prepared with essential healthcare information and safety tips can ensure a smooth and enjoyable journey. This chapter equips you with the knowledge and resources to navigate any potential health concerns and stay safe during your Vicenza adventure.

Healthcare:

Travel Insurance:

Importance: Consider purchasing comprehensive travel insurance before your trip. Travel insurance can provide coverage for medical emergencies, trip cancellations, or lost luggage, offering peace of mind during your travels.

Coverage: Choose a travel insurance plan that includes medical coverage for unexpected illnesses or injuries during your trip. Review the policy details to understand coverage limits and exclusions.

Pre-Existing Conditions: If you have any pre-existing medical conditions, ensure your travel insurance plan covers them. You might need to obtain a doctor's letter confirming your health status for coverage.

Medical Facilities:

Hospitals and Clinics: Vicenza boasts several reputable hospitals and clinics that provide quality medical care.

Public vs. Private: Italy operates a dual healthcare system with both public and private hospitals. Public hospitals require a European Health Insurance Card (EHIC) for EU citizens, while private hospitals cater to all patients, but might have higher fees.

Pharmacies: Pharmacies (farmacie in Italian) are easily identifiable by a green cross sign. Pharmacists can dispense basic medications and offer advice for minor ailments.

Before You Go:

Vaccinations: Ensure your vaccinations, including measles, mumps, rubella, tetanus, diphtheria, and hepatitis A and B, are up-to-date before your trip. Consult your doctor to determine if additional vaccinations are recommended for Italy.

Prescription Medications: Pack an adequate supply of any prescription medications you require for the duration of your trip. Carry a doctor's note explaining the medication and its purpose, especially if traveling with controlled substances.

Basic First-Aid Kit: Pack a compact first-aid kit containing essential items like bandages, antiseptic wipes, pain relievers, and any medications you might need.

Staying Healthy:

Sun Protection: Italy's Mediterranean climate boasts sunshine most of the year. Pack sunscreen with an SPF of 30 or higher and reapply frequently, especially during peak sun hours. Consider wearing a hat and sunglasses for additional protection.

Hydration: Staying hydrated is crucial, especially during hot weather. Carry a reusable water bottle and refill it frequently throughout the day. Tap water in Vicenza is generally safe to drink, but bottled water might be preferred by some travelers.

Food Safety: While Italian cuisine is renowned for its freshness and flavor, be mindful of food safety, especially during hot weather. Avoid street food that has been sitting out for extended periods and opt for freshly cooked meals. Choose restaurants with good hygiene practices.

Insect Repellent: Consider using insect repellent, particularly during summer months, to avoid mosquito bites and potential insect-borne illnesses.

Safety Tips:

Petty Theft: Vicenza is generally a safe city, but petty theft can occur, particularly in crowded areas like tourist attractions and public transportation. Be mindful of your belongings, especially wallets, purses, and phones. Avoid carrying large sums of cash and consider using a money belt or crossbody bag for added security.

Pickpockets: Be particularly cautious of pickpockets in crowded areas. Keep your valuables close to your body and avoid placing wallets or phones in easily accessible pockets like backpacks.

Scams: While uncommon, tourist scams can occasionally occur. Be wary of individuals offering unsolicited "help" or overly discounted goods or services. Trust your instincts and avoid situations that seem suspicious.

Traffic Safety: Italy follows a right-of-way system for pedestrians. Be cautious when crossing streets and pay attention to traffic signals. If renting a bicycle or scooter, familiarize yourself with local traffic regulations and wear a helmet for safety.

Emergency Numbers: Store essential emergency numbers in your phone, including the police (112), ambulance (118), and fire department (115).

Additional Tips:

Learn Basic Italian Phrases: Knowing a few basic Italian phrases can enhance communication and potentially help you avoid misunderstandings. It also demonstrates respect for the local culture.

Dress Modestly: When visiting religious sites, dress modestly with clothing that covers your shoulders and knees. A scarf is a handy solution for quick adjustments.

Respect Local Customs: Be mindful of local customs and traditions. Avoid speaking loudly in public places, especially churches or museums. Smoking is prohibited in most indoor spaces, including restaurants and public transportation.

Be Culturally Sensitive: Embrace the Italian way of life and avoid being overly critical of cultural differences. Patience and a friendly demeanor go a long way in fostering positive interactions with locals.

Trust Your Gut: If a situation feels unsafe, don't hesitate to remove yourself from it. Trust your instincts and prioritize your safety.

In Case of Emergency:

Stay Calm: If you encounter an emergency, remain calm and assess the situation.

Seek Help: Don't hesitate to seek help from bystanders or authorities. If you require medical attention, dial 118 for an ambulance. For police assistance, dial 112. If you speak limited Italian, try to find someone who can translate for you.

Contact Your Embassy: If you lose your passport or require further assistance, contact your nearest embassy or consulate. They can provide guidance and support during emergencies.

Useful Resources - Websites, apps, and local tourist information

Planning a trip to Vicenza, Italy, promises an unforgettable adventure. To ensure a smooth and enriching experience,having access to the right resources is crucial. This chapter equips you with a comprehensive list of websites, apps, and local tourist information sources to enhance your Vicenza exploration.

Essential Websites:

Vicenza Tourism Official Website:
https://www.vicenzae.org/en/297-english/tourism - This comprehensive website serves as your one-stop shop for all things Vicenza. Explore sections on attractions, events,accommodation, restaurants, and practical information like transportation and maps. It's available in multiple languages.

Italian National Tourism Agency (ENIT):
https://www.italia.it/en - ENIT provides a wealth of information on Italy as a whole, including a dedicated section for the Veneto region where Vicenza is located. Discover travel tips,regional highlights, and cultural insights.

Google Maps: https://maps.google.com/ - An essential tool for navigating Vicenza. Download offline maps before your trip to ensure accessibility even without internet connection. Use it to locate attractions, restaurants, and public transportation options.

TripAdvisor: https://www.tripadvisor.com/ - This popular platform offers user reviews, ratings, and recommendations for hotels, restaurants, attractions, and activities in Vicenza. Leverage the collective wisdom of fellow travelers to plan your itinerary.

The Local Italy: https://www.thelocal.it/ - Stay updated on current events, cultural happenings, and insider tips through this English-language website focused on Italy.

Helpful Mobile Apps:

Duolingo or Memrise: Learning a few basic Italian phrases can significantly enhance your experience. These language learning apps offer fun and interactive ways to build your Italian vocabulary.

Citymapper or Google Maps: Essential for navigating Vicenza's streets and public transportation system. These apps provide real-time directions, estimated travel times, and alternative routes.

WhatsApp: A popular messaging app widely used in Italy for communication. Download it to stay connected with friends, family, and potentially local contacts during your trip.

XE Currency Converter: Stay on top of exchange rates with this app that allows you to easily convert currencies.This can be helpful for budgeting and making informed financial decisions while traveling.

Rick Steves Audio Europe: Download self-guided audio tours for Vicenza and other Italian cities from Rick Steves. Explore at your own pace while learning about the city's history and landmarks. (fee-based app)

Local Tourist Information:

Vicenza Tourist Information Office: Located in the heart of the city, this office provides free maps, brochures,and expert advice on attractions, events, and transportation. Staff can answer your questions and help you plan your itinerary.

Accommodation Concierge: Most hotels and accommodations offer concierge services that can assist you with booking tours, recommending restaurants, and arranging transportation.

Local Museums and Attractions: Many museums and attractions in Vicenza have their own websites or social media pages. These resources provide detailed information about exhibitions, opening hours, and ticket prices.

Additional Resources:

Travel Blogs: Research travel blogs focused on Vicenza or Italy as a whole. Discover hidden gems, personalized recommendations, and unique perspectives from experienced travelers.

Travel Guidebooks: While guidebooks might seem old-fashioned in our digital age, they can be valuable resources for offline information access. Consider purchasing a reputable guidebook with detailed maps, historical insights,and recommendations for attractions and restaurants.

Language Learning Resources: Invest in a phrasebook or dictionary to have basic Italian phrases readily available during your trip. Many online language learning resources offer free or paid courses to help you learn basic Italian communication skills.

Embrace the Local Experience:

While these resources provide valuable information, don't be afraid to step off the beaten path and explore Vicenza independently. Engage with locals, ask for recommendations, and discover hidden gems not listed in guidebooks.Embrace the opportunity to learn about the city's culture and traditions firsthand.

Map of Vicenza

Vicenza, a captivating city nestled in Italy's Veneto region, boasts a rich history and a vibrant culture. To fully explore its treasures, having access to various maps is essential. This chapter provides an overview of the different maps available to enhance your Vicenza adventure.

City Map:

A detailed city map is fundamental for navigating Vicenza's streets, squares, and landmarks. These maps typically include:

Streets and alleys

Piazzas (squares)

Major landmarks and attractions

Public transportation routes

Points of interest (POIs) like museums, churches, and restaurants

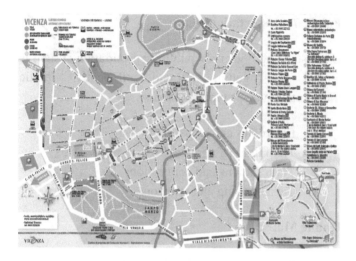

Tourist Map:

Tourist maps often highlight the city's must-see attractions, cultural gems, and popular tourist destinations. They might also include:

- Walking tours and suggested itineraries
- Information on museums, opening hours, and ticket prices
- Restaurant recommendations and nightlife hotspots
- Shopping districts and markets

Public Transportation Map:

Understanding Vicenza's public transportation system is crucial for getting around efficiently. Public transportation maps typically show:

- Bus routes and stops
- Tram lines (if applicable)
- Train stations and connections
- Ticket pricing and fare zones

Online Maps:

Numerous online map services like Google Maps and OpenStreetMap offer real-time navigation, street views, and user-generated reviews. These can be invaluable tools for finding specific locations, checking traffic conditions, and exploring off-the-beaten-path destinations.

Museum and Attraction Maps:

Many museums and attractions in Vicenza have their own maps that provide detailed layouts of their exhibits and collections. These maps can help you plan your visit and ensure you don't miss any highlights.

CONCLUSIONS

Your Vicenza adventure awaits! This captivating city, steeped in Renaissance charm and pulsating with contemporary energy, promises an unforgettable journey. As you embark on your exploration, the knowledge and resources gathered throughout this book will serve as your trusted companion.

A Treasure Trove of Experiences:

Vicenza's historical significance unfolds through its architectural marvels, from the majestic Basilica Palladiana to the elegant Teatro Olimpico. Delve into the artistic legacy of Andrea Palladio, whose architectural genius continues to inspire.Beyond the iconic landmarks, hidden piazzas and charming streets beckon, waiting to be discovered.

A Culinary Adventure:

Indulge in the culinary delights that define Vicenza. Savor fresh, seasonal ingredients crafted into delectable dishes like Bigoli con l'Anatra (duck sauce pasta) and Baccalà alla Vicentina (codfish stew). Pair your meals with local wines from the Veneto region and experience the true essence of Italian gastronomy.

A Cultural Tapestry:

Vicenza's vibrant culture offers a glimpse into the Italian way of life. Immerse yourself in bustling markets, witness the passion of a local football match, or participate in a traditional festival. Engage with friendly locals and learn about their rich heritage and customs.

More Than Just a City:

Vicenza serves as a gateway to the Veneto region's diverse landscape. Explore the rolling hills of the Prosecco wine region, discover the beauty of Lake Garda, or venture to the charming city of Verona. Vicenza's central location offers a convenient base for exploring the broader region.

A Journey of Self-Discovery:

Beyond the sightseeing and culinary experiences, Vicenza offers a journey of self-discovery. Embrace the opportunity to slow down, appreciate the beauty of everyday life, and connect with a different culture. Create lasting memories, capture experiences through photos and stories, and return home with a renewed perspective.

A Lasting Impact:

Vicenza's magic lies not just in its historical treasures but also in its ability to captivate the senses and touch the soul. As you depart, you'll carry a piece of Vicenza with you – a newfound appreciation for art, architecture, and the simple joys of life.

Final Tips:

- **Embrace the Unexpected:** Leave room for spontaneity and unexpected discoveries. Vicenza offers hidden gems waiting to be unveiled around every corner.
- **Be a Responsible Traveler:** Respect local customs, dress modestly when visiting religious sites, and dispose of waste responsibly.
- **Learn a Few Italian Phrases:** Even a few basic Italian phrases can enhance your communication and demonstrate respect for the local culture.
- **Connect with Locals:** Engage with friendly locals, ask questions, and discover their perspectives on their city.
- **Savor the Moment:** Take time to appreciate the beauty of Vicenza, savor the local cuisine, and create lasting memories.

The Adventure Begins:

With this comprehensive guide in hand, you are well-equipped to navigate the streets of Vicenza, discover its hidden treasures, and experience its unique charm. So, pack your bags, embrace the adventure, and prepare to unveil the magic of Vicenza!

Beyond the Guidebook:

This guidebook serves as a starting point for your Vicenza adventure. Remember, the most enriching experiences often lie beyond the pages. Don't be afraid to venture off the beaten path, explore independently, and create your own unique Vicenza story. Buon viaggio (have a good trip) and arrivederci (goodbye) until we meet again in the captivating city of Vicenza!

APPENDIX

This appendix serves as a quick reference guide for essential information to enhance your trip to Vicenza, Italy.

Getting There:

Airports: The closest major airport to Vicenza is Venice Marco Polo Airport (VCE). Several airlines offer flights to Venice from various international destinations. From Venice, you can connect to Vicenza by train or bus.Alternatively, Verona Villafranca Airport (VRN) might offer flight options depending on your origin city.

Trains: Italy boasts an extensive train network. High-speed trains connect major cities like Milan, Rome, and Florence to Vicenza. For regional connections and slower but scenic journeys, consider local trains.

Buses: Bus travel within Italy is a budget-friendly option. Several long-distance bus companies connect Vicenza to other Italian cities and European destinations.

Getting Around:

Walking: Vicenza's historic center is compact and easily walkable, allowing you to explore the main attractions at your own pace. Comfortable walking shoes are highly recommended.

Bicycles: Vicenza offers a bike-sharing program, allowing you to rent bicycles for a convenient and eco-friendly way to explore the city.

Public Transportation: Vicenza's public transportation system consists of buses and trams. Purchase tickets in advance from authorized retailers or onboard designated machines.

Taxis: Taxis are readily available in major squares and tourist areas. Agree on the fare beforehand to avoid misunderstandings.

Currency and Money Exchange:

Currency: Italy uses the Euro (EUR). Before your trip, research current exchange rates and consider exchanging some currency to euros in advance.

ATMs: ATMs are widely available throughout Vicenza, allowing you to withdraw cash using your debit or credit card. Be aware of potential fees associated with international ATM withdrawals.

Credit Cards: Most major credit cards are widely accepted in Vicenza, particularly at hotels, restaurants, and tourist shops. However, it's always wise to carry some cash for smaller purchases or emergencies.

Visas and Immigration:

Visa Requirements: Citizens from most European Union (EU) countries do not require a visa to enter Italy for short stays. Non-EU citizens should check visa requirements with the nearest Italian embassy or consulate before their trip.

Passport: Ensure your passport has at least six months of validity remaining from your planned date of departure from Italy.

Time Zone:

Time Zone: Italy observes Central European Time (CET), which is one hour ahead of Coordinated Universal Time (UTC) and six hours ahead of Pacific Standard Time (PST) during winter months. During Daylight Saving Time (DST), Italy is two hours ahead of UTC and seven hours ahead of PST.

Electricity:

Voltage: Italy uses a standard voltage of 230 volts AC at 50 hertz (Hz). If you're traveling from a country with a different voltage, you will need a voltage converter to use your electronic devices.

Plug Type: Italy uses the Europlug (Type C) two-pronged plug with round pins. Invest in a universal travel adapter to ensure compatibility with your electronic devices.

Important Phone Numbers:

Emergency Services: 112 (Police), 118 (Ambulance), 115 (Fire Department)

Tourist Information: +39 0444 320 700

Opening Hours and Holidays:

Shops: Most shops typically open from 9:00 AM to 1:00 PM and 4:00 PM to 7:30 PM, with a longer lunch break in the afternoon. On Sundays, most shops are closed, except for some tourist shops in major areas.

Museums: Opening hours for museums and attractions can vary. Research specific opening times and potential closure days before your visit.

National Holidays: Major national holidays in Italy include New Year's Day, Easter Monday, Liberation Day (April 25), Republic Day (June 2), Assumption of Mary (August 15), All Saints' Day (November 1), and Christmas Day (December 25). Many businesses and attractions might have adjusted opening hours on these days.

Additional Resources:

- **Italian National Tourism Agency (ENIT):** https://www.italia.it/en
- **Vicenza Tourism Official Website:** [https://www.vicenzae.org/en/297-english/touris m](https://www.vicenzae.org/en/

ABOUT THE AUTHOR

Garfield James is a seasoned traveler with an insatiable curiosity for exploring the world's hidden corners and vibrant cultures. His passion for travel extends beyond simply visiting new places; it's a deep-rooted desire to understand the essence of a destination, to connect with its people, and to capture its unique spirit.

James' background is multifaceted, drawing upon experiences in various fields. This diverse perspective allows him to craft travel guides that are informative, engaging, and go beyond the superficial. He delves into the historical, cultural,and social fabric of a destination, providing readers with a well-rounded understanding that enriches their travel experience.

Driven by a desire to share his travel insights and inspire others to explore, James turned his passion into prose. His writing style is both informative and evocative, transporting readers to the heart of the destinations he explores. He weaves together practical information with captivating storytelling, ensuring his guides are not just resources but also captivating reads.

Beyond his published works, Garfield James is an active speaker and travel advocate. He frequently shares his travel experiences and insights through lectures, workshops, and online platforms. His infectious enthusiasm and genuine love for exploration encourage others to step outside their comfort zones and discover the world for themselves.

A Commitment to Sustainable Travel

Garfield James is a strong advocate for responsible and sustainable travel practices. He encourages readers to minimize their environmental impact, support local communities, and respect the cultural heritage of the destinations they visit. His guides offer tips on responsible travel practices, ensuring that travelers leave a positive footprint wherever they go.

A Window into the World

Garfield James' travel guides are more than just trip itineraries; they are invitations to embark on a journey of discovery.By delving into the hidden gems, local traditions, and captivating stories of a place, his work allows readers to experience the world in a new and meaningful way. So, whether you're an armchair traveler or a seasoned adventurer, Garfield James' work is sure to inspire you to explore the world with a curious mind and an open heart.

Made in United States
Troutdale, OR
11/22/2024

25189426R00060